Talking About Time

Times of the Day

Jilly Attwood

Chicago, Illinois

Published by Raintree, a division of Reed Elsevier, Inc.
Chicago, Illinois
Customer Service 888-363-4266
Visit our website at www.raintreelibrary.com

For information, address the publisher:
Raintree, 100 N. LaSalle, Suite 1200, Chicago, IL 60602

Printed and bound by South China Printing Company.
09 08 07 06 05
10 9 8 7 6 5 4 3 2 1

Library of Congress Cataloging-in-Publication Data:
Attwood, Jilly.
Talking about time : times of the day / Jilly Attwood.
p. cm.
ISBN 1-4109-1641-3 (library binding-hardcover) -- ISBN 1-4109-1647-2 (pbk.) 1. Day--Juvenile literature. 2. Time--Juvenile literature. I. Title.
QB209.5.A88 2005
525'.35--dc22
2004025609

Acknowledgments
The publishers would like to thank the following for permission to reproduce photographs: Corbis p. **13**; Corbis/RF p. **5**; Getty Images/Photodisc pp. **14**, **16**; Harcourt Education pp. **4**, **9**, **18a**, **18b** (Tudor Photography), **6**, **15**, **17** (Trevor Clifford), **7**, **10**, **12**, **19**, **20**, **21** (Gareth Boden), **11** (Martin Sookias), **15** (Anthony King); John Walmsley p. **8**.

Cover photograph reproduced with permission of Harcourt Education (Gareth Boden).

Some words are shown in bold, **like this**. You can find out what they mean by looking in the glossary on page 24.

Contents

It's Morning!

Rise and shine!

It's time to get up.
It's time to get dressed.

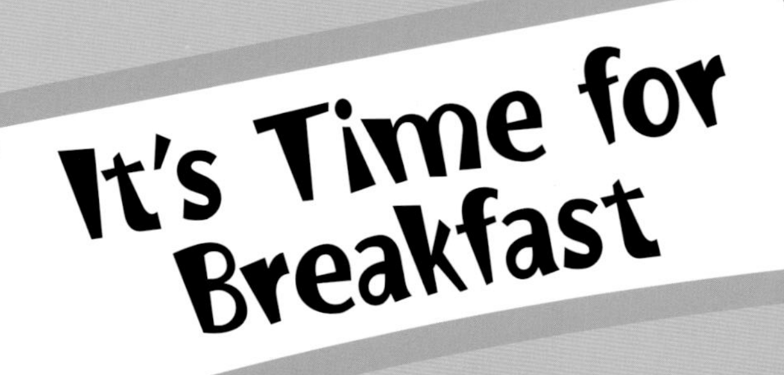

It's Time for Breakfast

What do you eat for **breakfast**?

Brush, brush,
brush!
It's time
to brush
your teeth.

It's Time to Go

It's time to go to school.

How do you get to school?

It's also time to go to work.

It's School Time

It's time
to paint.
Do you like
to paint?

Splat

It's time to read!

What is your favorite story?

It's Lunch Time

It's time for lunch.

After lunch it's time to play.

Hooray!

After School Time

What do you like to do after school?

11
TABBY

It's Dinner Time

It's time to make **dinner**.

Do you help to make dinner?

What is your favorite food for dinner?

It's Fun Time

What do you do after dinner?

Senses
Seeing in Living Things
Senses
Seeing
in Living Things

It's Bed Time

It's time to get ready for bed.

It's time to brush your teeth again.

Time for sleep.
Goodnight!

What's The Time?

Glossary

breakfast a meal eaten in the beginning of the day
dinner a meal eaten at the end of the day
lunch a meal eaten in the middle of the day

Index

Notes for adults

The *Talking about time* series introduces young children to the concept of time. By relating their own experiences to specific moments in time, the children can start to explore the pattern of regular events that occur in a day, week or year.

This book shows the significant events that take place in most children's lives over the course of a day. The events are given in chronological order to aid children's thought about the passing of time during the day. The book encourages children to discuss why something happens at a particular time of day. Simple clock times introduce children to the conventional way of showing time.

Follow-up activities
Draw the events that your child experiences during a day of the week on separate note cards. Mix up the cards and ask the child to place them in the correct time sequence, while discussing what happens before and after each event.
Throughout the day, incidentally point out hour times on a clock and link them with important landmarks that occur in the morning, afternoon and at night.